Philosophy for children

From child to children

Once upon a time!

How big is daddy from heaven!

Coloring story!

By: Bernardo Octaviano Pereira

This book belongs to:

____

I dedicate this work, firstly, to my parents who I love so much, to my teachers, to my dear aunts and to all my friends, may God bless you all infinitely!

Bernardo Octaviano Pereira

16/04/2024

Once upon a time, in a house near here, a curious little boy asked his daddy:

- Daddy, how big is daddy in heaven, Daddy, facing the difficult task of explaining something so abstract, faced with such a challenging question, daddy observed the sky for a few moments.

Upon seeing a plane passing in the distance, the father had an idea to explain to his little son. That was when he looked up at the sky and saw a plane passing very far away, and he spoke to his little son;

- See that plane passing in the sky, that's the size of Daddy in the sky! And the little son having a lot of trouble seeing the plane,

because he was
too far away,
he said to his
daddy;
- But daddy, is
daddy in
heaven that
small?

And dad, noticing his little son's difficulty in seeing the distant plane in the sky, decided to act. He invited his little son to accompany him and, together, they went to the airport.

Arriving there, next to an imposing aircraft, dad asked again:
- And now how big is it? The little son, impressed by the size of the plane, said;
- Wow, daddy, he's very big, he's too big, he's huge.

The little son, now marveling at the size of the plane before his eyes, began to understand the metaphor better. "I understand dad! Heavenly Father is like that plane, big and powerful, but in a way that goes beyond what the eyes can see."

And the father, satisfied with having conveyed the message, smiled at his little son and said: "Exactly, my son, your heavenly father is immeasurable, not just in size, but in love, care and constant presence.

- Well, that's how daddy in heaven is, the further you get away from him, the further away you are from him, the smaller he seems;

Better with God than without him. Never turn away from God, so you don't regret it later

The end!